SPARKNOTES
Power
Tactics
FOR THE NEW SAT

THE NEW SAT
TEST-TAKING STRATEGIES

SPARK
NOTES

A DIVISION OF BARNES & NOBLE PUBLISHING

SPARKNOTES is a registered trademark of SparkNotes LLC

Spark Educational Publishing
A Division of Barnes & Noble Publishing
120 Fifth Avenue
New York, NY 10011

ISBN 1-4114-0281-2

Please submit changes or report errors to *www.sparknotes.com/errors*.

Printed and bound in Canada.

SAT is the registered trademark of the College Entrance Examination Board, which was not involved in the production of, and does not endorse this product.

Written by Doug Tarnopol

CONTENTS

The Power Tactics 15

The Practice Sets 49

INTRODUCTION

Truly effective SAT preparation doesn't need to be painful or time consuming. SparkNotes' *Power Tactics for the New SAT* is proof that powerful test preparation can be streamlined so that you study only what you need. Instead of toiling away through a 700-page book or an expensive six-week course, you can choose the *Power Tactics* book that gets you where you want to be a lot sooner.

Perhaps you're Kid Math, the fastest number-slinger this side of the Mississippi, but a bit of a bumbler when it comes to words. Or maybe you've got the verbal parts down but can't seem to manage algebraic functions. SparkNotes' *Power Tactics for the New SAT* provides an extremely focused review of every component on the new SAT, so you can design your own program of study.

If you're not exactly sure where you fall short, log on to **testprep.sparknotes.com/powertactics** and take our free diagnostic SAT test. This test will pinpoint your weaknesses and reveal exactly where to focus.

Since you're holding this book in your hands, it's pretty likely that you need some test-taking strategies to guide your study and preparation for the SAT. You've made the right decision because in a few short hours, you will have mastered the art of taking the SAT. No sweat, no major investment of time or money, no problem.

So, let's not waste any time: go forth and conquer the SAT so you can get on with the *better parts* of your life!

A USER'S GUIDE

Reading this book will provide you with powerful strategies to maximize your score on the SAT. To achieve your target score, you'll learn:

- About the new SAT—how it's structured and scored
- Global test-taking strategies
- Targeted strategies for each section of the test
- How to apply these strategies to real SAT questions
- How to build a study plan for the SAT
- How to conquer test anxiety

As you have no doubt been told, the SAT does not measure your IQ or how smart you are. More than anything, it is a test of how good you are at taking the SAT. This book is designed to arm you with strategies that are specifically targeted toward *taking the test*. These techniques are powerful tools that will enable you to approach the test "strategically," ensuring that you reach your target score.

At the same time, the SAT does test certain discrete concepts. For example, you are not going to score high on the Math section if you don't have certain algebraic concepts down cold, such as "absolute value" or "functions," despite any SAT tricks or tips you may have under your belt.

To get the most of out of this book, go to **testprep.sparknotes.com/ powertactics** for a free full-length diagnostic **pretest**. This test can will point out your strengths and weaknesses for the entire SAT and point you toward one of the other *Power Tactic* books in this series, should you need to review any essential concepts.

ABOUT THE NEW SAT

Journalists always aim to dig out answers to the Five Ws: who, what, where, when, why. *How* is usually added to this list. This book aims to answer all these questions about the SAT.

We break this section into two parts. In the first part, "Anatomy of the Test," we describe what the SAT is made of and what the test-makers are trying to find out about you. We answer the *what* and *why* questions:

- What is this test?
- Why has it changed?
- What content is tested?
- What is its structure?

In the second part, "Taking the Test," we answer the *how*, *when*, and *where* questions:

- How do I register?
- When should I take it?
- Where should I take it?
- How often should I take it?

What about the *who*? Well, the *who* is you. You are the test-taker. This book guides your preparation for the SAT by giving you targeted, strategic advice.

THE OLD

The SAT, first administered in 1926, has undergone a thorough restructuring. For the last ten years, the SAT consisted of two sections: Verbal and Math. The Verbal section contained Analogies, Sentence Completions, and Critical Reading passages and questions. The Math section tested arithmetic, algebra, and geometry, as well as some probability, statistics, and data interpretation.

You received one point for each correct answer. For most questions, a quarter of a point was deducted for each incorrect answer. This was called the "wrong-answer penalty," which was designed to neutralize random guessing. If you simply filled in the bubble sheet at random, you'd likely get one-fifth of the items correct, given that each item has five answer choices (excluding student-produced–response items). You'd also get four-fifths of the items wrong, losing $4 \times 1/4$, or 1 point for the four incorrectly answered items. Every time you determined an answer choice was wrong, you'd improve your odds by beating the wrong-answer penalty. The net number of points (less wrong-answer penalties) was called the "raw score."

Raw score = # of correct answers – ($1/4$ × # of wrong answers)

That score was then converted to the familiar 200–800 "scaled score."

THE NEW

For 2005, the SAT added a Writing section and an essay, changed the name of *Verbal* to *Critical Reading*, and has added algebra II content to the Math section. The following chart compares the old SAT with the new SAT:

Old SAT	New SAT
Verbal	**Critical Reading**
Analogies	*Eliminated*
Sentence Completions	Sentence Completions
Long Reading Passages	Long Reading Passages
Paired Reading Passages	Paired Reading Passages
	Short Reading Passages
Math—Question Types	
Multiple Choice	Multiple Choice
Quantitative Comparisons	*Eliminated*
Student-produced Responses	Student-produced Responses
Math—Content Areas	
Numbers & Operations	Numbers & Operations
Algebra I	Algebra I
	Algebra II
Geometry	Geometry
Data Analysis, Statistics & Probability	Data Analysis, Statistics & Probability
	Writing
	Identifying Sentence Errors
	Improving Sentences
	Improving Paragraphs
	Essay
Total Time: 3 hours	*Total Time*: 3 hours, 45 minutes
Maximum Scaled Score: 1600	*Maximum Scaled Score*: 2400 Separate Essay Score (2–12)

The scoring for the test is the same, except that the Writing section provides a third 200–800 scaled score, and there is now a separate essay score. The wrong-answer penalty is still in effect.

NEW PACKAGE, OLD PRODUCT

While the test has changed for test-*takers*, it has not changed all that much from the test-*maker*'s point of view. The Educational Testing Service (ETS) is a nonprofit institute that creates the SAT for The College Board. Test creation is not as simple a task as you might think. Any standardized test question has to go through a rigorous series of editorial reviews and statistical studies before it can be released to the public. In fact, that's why the old SAT featured a seventh, unscored, "experimental" section: new questions were introduced and tested out in these sections. ETS "feeds" potential questions to its test-takers to measure the level of difficulty. Given the complex and lengthy process of developing new questions, it would be impossible for ETS to introduce *totally* new question types or make major changes to existing question types.

Now that you know these facts, the "new" SAT will start to make more sense. The changes were neither random nor unexpected. Actually, the only truly *new* question type on the SAT is the short reading passage followed by a couple of questions. However, the skills tested and strategies required are virtually identical to the tried-and-true long reading-passage question type. All other additions to the test consist of new *content* rather than new *question types*. Both multiple-choice and student-produced–response math questions ("grid-ins") will now feature algebra II concepts. Same question type, new content. Critical Reading features one fiction passage per tests, as well as questions on genre, rhetorical devices, and cause and effect. Same question type, different content.

Even the much-feared new Writing section is in a sense old news. Both the PSAT and the SAT II Writing test have featured exactly the same multiple-choice question types for years. The essay format and scoring rubric are virtually identical to those of the SAT II Writing test. The College Board had no other choice, given how long the test-development process is.

The other major changes are omissions, not additions: Quantitative Comparisons and Analogies have been dumped from the test.

So in a nutshell, ETS has simply attached an SAT II Writing test to the old SAT, dropped Analogies and Quantitative Comparisons, added some algebra II content and short reading passages, and ensured that some fiction and fiction-related questions are included. That's it.

READING AND WRITING ON THE NEW SAT

The English language is made up of several building blocks that give meaning to what you read and write. From smallest to largest, they are:

- Words
- Phrases and Clauses
- Sentences
- Paragraphs
- Passages

In this list, each level contains the elements above it. For example, you can't have a paragraph without sentences.

The Critical Reading and Writing sections test each building block in a complementary way. When you master one question type, you're actually laying the groundwork for the other items on these two sections.

THE NEW CRITICAL READING SECTION

The new Critical Reading section consists of Sentence Completions and Reading Passages. In this section, your job is to *recognize* the correct use of language:

- **Sentence Completions** test the conventions of grammar, proper use of vocabulary, and common-sense logic at the sentence level. Word choice, phrases, and clauses—the building blocks of sentences—are tested as well.
- **Reading Passages** test not only the sentence-level conventions listed above but also style, genre, argumentation, and plot, which really occur only at the paragraph or passage level.

THE NEW MULTIPLE-CHOICE WRITING SECTION

Instead of testing your ability to recognize the rules, conventions, and features of *good* writing, the Writing section's multiple-choice questions test whether you can *apply* these conventions to *poor* writing.

- **Sentence Error IDs** require you to identify an error, if one exists, at the sentence level.

- **Sentence Improvements** require you not only to identify an error at the sentence level but also to choose the best way to fix that error.
- **Paragraph Improvements** require you to identify and fix errors not only at the sentence level but also at the paragraph and passage level.

THE NEW ESSAY

Finally, the **essay** tests how well you can organize all of your language skills to *generate* a well-constructed written argument in a short amount of time.

INTERTWINED SKILLS

Each Critical Reading and Writing item type attacks the conventions of language from a slightly different angle, as the following chart summarizes:

Section	Question Type	Focus	Primary Features Tested	How Tested
Critical Reading	Sentence Completions	Words, phrases, clauses, sentences	Vocabulary and word choice, grammar, logic	You must *recognize* rules of language in well-written sentences
Critical Reading	Short, Paired, and Long Reading Passages	Sentences, paragraphs, passages	All of the above, but emphasis on style, genre, and the logic of argumentation and scenario development	You must *recognize* rules of language in well-written paragraphs and passages

Section	Question Type	Focus	Primary Features Tested	How Tested
Writing	Identifying Sentence Errors and Improving Sentences	Words, phrases, clauses, sentences	Vocabulary and word choice, grammar, logic	You must *apply* good writing to poorly written sentences
	Improving Paragraphs	Sentences, paragraphs, passages	All of the above, but emphasis on style, genre, and the logic of argument-ation and scenario de-velopment	You must *apply* good writing to poorly written paragraphs
	Essay	Words, phrases, clauses, sentences, paragraphs, passages	Vocabulary, word choice, grammar, logic, style, organization, the logic of argumentation	You must *create* well-written, clearly constructed piece of writing

By learning to answer Sentence Completions, you are reviewing how well-written sentences are constructed. This helps you when you turn to Identifying Sentence Errors and Improving Sentences. As you read well-written Short Reading Passages and answer questions on their structure, you are gaining valuable insights for Improving Paragraphs. Similarly, as you read well-written long and paired Reading Passages and answer questions on their organization, you are provided with excellent models and insights you can use when the time comes for you to write your own Essay. This works in the other direction as well: preparing for the Writing section will reinforce your Critical Reading preparation.

MATH ON THE NEW SAT

On the Math section, there are fewer question types: multiple choice and grid-ins. These items are nearly the same. Multiple choice has answer choices, and grid-ins do not. The key divisions in math are really based on content areas: numbers and operations; algebra; geometry; and data analysis, statistics and probability.

The Math section still tests critical thinking as much as do the Critical Reading and Writing sections. Sure, you must master the essential math concepts so that your "tool box" is full when you encounter an item. But, you also need to *think* as you work through the Math sections. The SAT tests how you can *apply* the proper concepts quickly to solve problems.

Mastering the essential math concepts is necessary but not enough. You must also master the strategies that will get you thinking like an efficient problem-solver.

TAKING THE TEST

When Should I Take the SAT?

Ideally, you should first take the SAT some time during your junior year of high school. That way, if you're not happy with your score, you can retake the test early in your senior year before college applications are due.

Exactly when to take the SAT during your junior year depends on many factors:

- How ready are you? Your scores on practice tests will help guide this decision.
- What other responsibilities do you have during the year? Jobs? Sports? Coursework? Finals, midterms, or other big tests? How will these obligations affect your state of mind? They might focus rather than distract you—only you will know.
- What other tests are you taking? APs and SAT IIs are often scheduled during the same time of year as the SAT. Trust us, you don't want to take the SAT *and* another test on the same day.

How Do I Register for the SAT?

You have a few options:

- Register online at **http://www.collegeboard.com/student/testing/sat/reg.html**.
- Register by mail by getting the official *Registration Bulletin* at your high school's guidance office.
- Register by phone (only if you've taken the SAT at least once already). Read all about it at **http://www.collegeboard.com/student/testing/sat/regPhone.html**.

Taking the new SAT will cost you $41.50. Financial aid is available for qualified students. You can find information on getting a fee waiver at: **http://www.collegeboard.com/student/testing/sat/calenfees/feewaivers.html**.

You can also find information on special circumstances for test-takers on the general College Board registration site.

How Many Times Should I Take the SAT?

Ideally, you'll take the test once and match or exceed your target score. If this doesn't happen, you should take several things into consideration:

- How far off your target score are you? We discuss target scores in a later section.
- How will colleges interpret multiple scores? Some schools average all your test scores, others take your most recent scores, and still others take the highest score from each section across different tests. The best way to find out is to call each school's admissions office.
- What impact will restudying have on your college applications? On your schoolwork and grades? On other standardized tests? Remember, the SAT is only one criterion for college admission.

THE POWER
TACTICS

TACKLING THE WHOLE TEST

Before diving into our global test-taking strategies, let's define some terms. We'll use an example from the multiple-choice portion of the Writing section:

6. Eager to pass his final exams, <u>studying was the student's top priority</u>.

(A) studying was the student's top priority.
(B) the student made studying his top priority.
(C) the top priority of the student was studying.
(D) the student's top priority was studying.
(E) studying was the top priority for the student.

The entire unit shown above is the **item**. The sentence containing the underlined portion is the **stem.** In a Math section item, the stem might be a word problem or a picture and question. The lettered options beneath the stem are the **answer choices**. Only one of the answer choices is correct. The other four answer choices are called **distractors** because that is exactly what they are designed to do—*distract* attention from the correct answer.

In Reading Passages and Paragraph Improvement, you'll also have **passages** that provide information. In those item types, more than one item is tied to a passage. The passage plus items is called a **set**. A set can also be a group of items that aren't tied to passages, such as a bunch of Sentence Completions in a Critical Reading section or algebra items in a Math section.

A **section** refers to a Critical Reading, Writing, or Math timed section that usually contains a mix of various item types.

BOMBING RUNS

The key to tackling any standardized test is managing your time so you can answer as many items correctly as possible. On just about every test you take in school, you start at number 1, work on it until you come up with an answer, go to number 2, do the same, and so on. This method is *death* on the SAT, and here's why. Imagine two test-takers, Jack and Jill, who have identical skill levels. Each test-taker has the ability to answer every item on an SAT set correctly. The set has ten items, in the following order of difficulty:

Item Number	Difficulty Level
1	Hard
2	Easy
3	Hard
4	Easy
5	Hard
6	Medium
7	Easy
8	Easy
9	Medium
10	Hard

Jack follows human nature. He starts at the first question and works his way through the set in the order in which the items are presented, spending as much time to get an answer as is necessary. Jack runs out of time after item 6, but he gets all six items correct.

Jill, however, flies **Bombing Runs**. She scans the items and completes the set in the following order:

Item Number	Order in Which Jill Attempts Item	Difficulty Level
1	7th	Hard
2	1st	Easy
3	8th	Hard
4	2nd	Easy
5	9th	Hard
6	5th	Medium
7	3rd	Easy
8	4th	Easy
9	6th	Medium
10	10th	Hard

Here's how Bombing Runs work: Jill does all the easy items first, then goes back and does all the medium items, and finally attempts the hard items. Jill—who has the exact same skill levels as Jack—has enough time to attempt every item on the set and gets all 10 points. Jill bombs the easy targets first, then the medium ones, and finally the hard ones.

Jill's got the right idea. Fly Bombing Runs to distribute your knowledge across a section as efficiently as possible.

Order of Difficulty

Easy, medium, hard—what do these terms really mean? Well, there are several ways of understanding difficulty on the SAT.

First, an item's difficulty is a statistical quality based on the test-takers who encountered that item on an experimental section. A geometry item can be considered hard if only those students who tend to score high in the Math section answer it correctly.

The items in Sentence Completion sets and multiple-choice Math sections are set up by order of difficulty, whereas the other sections mix these items up. More difficult items tend to have more seductive distractors.

But you're an individual, and just because *most* test-takers found an item easy (or hard) doesn't mean that *you* will. When you fly Bombing Runs and skip around in a section, your personal determination of an item's difficulty based on your experience and practice is what counts, not its statistical difficulty level. Difficulty is *not* an essential feature of an item.

The take-home message here is not to worry too much about how the SAT orders the items on a set. What counts is *your* order of difficulty.

We illustrate this in the chart below. Jack and Jill have equivalent overall general skill levels—over a full test, they'll score the same—but more realistically, they have different specific skill levels. For example, Jack is better at geometry. Jill shines in word problems. Assume Jack and Jill are taking the same test but they categorize the difficulty of each item differently, as follows:

Item Number	Jack's Determination of Difficulty Level	Jill's Determination of Difficulty Level
1	Hard	Easy
2	Easy	Medium
3	Hard	Easy
4	Easy	Easy
5	Hard	Medium
6	Medium	Hard
7	Easy	Medium
8	Easy	Medium
9	Medium	Hard
10	Hard	Hard

As long as both Jack and Jill fly Bombing Runs, given that their overall skill levels are the same, we can assume they'll each answer all ten items correctly, although they'll attempt them in different orders, based on their own personal determination of difficulty level:

Item Number	Jack's Difficulty Level	Order in Which Jack Attempts Item	Jill's Difficulty Level	Order in Which Jill Attempts Item
1	Hard	7th	Easy	1st
2	Easy	1st	Medium	4th
3	Hard	8th	Easy	2nd
4	Easy	2nd	Easy	3rd
5	Hard	9th	Medium	5th
6	Medium	5th	Hard	8th

Item Number	Jack's Difficulty Level	Order in Which Jack Attempts Item	Jill's Difficulty Level	Order in Which Jill Attempts Item
7	Easy	3rd	Medium	6th
8	Easy	4th	Medium	7th
9	Medium	6th	Hard	9th
10	Hard	10th	Hard	10th

For any set, do the items in order of difficulty from easiest (for you) to hardest (for you). Ignore the order in which the items are presented. Smart test-takers fly Bombing Runs based on their personal determination of difficulty.

Section-Level Bombing Runs

We've been talking about flying Bombing Runs on sets of items, but you can also apply this strategy to an entire timed section. This strategy works especially well on the Critical Reading section. A typical Critical Reading section includes Sentence Completions, Short Reading Passage sets, and Long Reading Passage sets. Let's say you encountered a Critical Reading section made up of the following:

- 10 Sentence Completions.
- 1 Short Reading Passage on humanities with two items.
- 1 Short Reading Passage on science with two items.
- 1 Long fiction passage with nine items.

Because all items are worth the same amount of points, always do the lowest investment items first. Here's how you'd fly a Bombing Run on this section:

- Do the Sentence Completions first. They require a far lower time investment than the Reading Passages.
- Next, tackle the Short Reading Passages. They require less of an investment than the long passages. If you're into science, do that one first. If not, do the humanities one first.
- Tackle the long Reading Passage last, making sure to fly a Bombing Run within the *set* of items.

The same idea applies to the Math section. If you know you're good at geometry, word problems, or data analysis, do those items first.

Knowing When to Bail

If an item starts eating up a lot of time, you have to overcome your desire to finish at all costs. If you're taking too much time on an item, you'll eventually have to let go and move on. Items are each worth 1 point. You get no extra credit for taking five minutes to answer the hardest item on the test. Instead, you'll end up with 1 point and less time for all the easier items.

Bailing can mean a couple of things:

* Stopping work on that item completely and moving on to another item. You'll go back to it later if you have time.
* Eliminating one or more answer choices, guessing from the remaining, and moving on.

Keep a clock going in the back of your head as you work through a section. It doesn't pay to be too nutty about exact amounts of time, but if you're pushing two minutes for any item, you should be looking for a parachute—a way to bail out.

Think of it this way: don't be a drum machine or metronome, counting out exact packets of time per item. Be more like a real, human drummer, keeping time loosely. Through practice, you'll get a sense of how long it normally takes you to answer an item. Eventually, you will have the time constraints running in the back of your mind, but your focus will be on the item at hand, not the clock.

ACCURACY

Managing your time efficiently is only one part of the equation. Once you've got a plan for dealing with the set, you need execute that plan with accuracy. The more accurate you are, the more points you earn on the SAT. Here are some general tips that you should always keep in mind.

Have an Idea of the Answer Before You Look at Any Answer Choices

Remember, in multiple-choice items, four answer choices are *distractors*. Do *not* simply let the answer choices guide your thought. Attack each item with some idea of the correct answer. The methods you'll use for coming up with your own answer will differ for each item type. The other books in this *Power Tactics* series cover these methods in detail.

Avoid Carelessness

Speed is only part of the goal on the SAT. Speed balanced with accuracy is the full goal. In general, the less you do in your head and the more explicit you make your approach to every item, the less careless you'll be. If you're solving a math item, take the time to write out all your steps. Even an easy item can become a real challenge if you try to keep all the steps in your head.

In almost every situation, you'll also want to take a split-second and ask yourself the question, Is my answer reasonable? If not, chances are you made a careless mistake in solving the item.

Give the Item What It Wants.

This may seem most applicable to Math, but it's actually applicable to the entire test. In Math, you can be sure that a multistep item will include a distractor that lists a key number you need to find the ultimate result. For example, if an item asks you to solve for $x + 1$, you can be sure that the value of x will be one of the distractors. When you come up with an answer, make sure it's what the item is asking for. Usually on the SAT, you have to perform one final step to convert the number you've come up with into the number the item asks for.

All of Critical Reading—Sentence Completions and Reading Passages—tests your reading *in context*. So you may find distractors that are correct outside of the specific context but are actually incorrect in the item. For example, on some vocabulary items, the correct answer is usually a second or third meaning of the word. The context of the item determines which meaning is appropriate.

The Writing section is also context-dependent. You either identify an error (Identifying Sentence Errors) or identify an error and fix it (Improving Sentences and Paragraphs) according to the context of the sentence or sentences. Even the essay follows this guideline—one of the only ways to get a zero on the essay is not to address the issue presented in the prompt.

Educated Guessing

The SAT does *not* have a guessing penalty. What it does have is a **wrong-answer penalty**. The SAT is set up to cancel out random guessing, not educated guessing.

Here's an illustration. Imagine a ten-item set on the SAT. Each item has five answer choices, **A** through **E**. Let's say you simply fill in the bubble sheet randomly. For every item you get right, you get a point. For every item you get wrong, you lose a quarter-point. What would happen?

Item	Right Answer	Your Random Guess	Right/Wrong	Points Gained or Lost
1	D	A	Wrong	−1/4
2	C	B	Wrong	−1/4
3	B	C	Wrong	−1/4
4	A	D	Wrong	−1/4
5	D	D	Right	+1
6	D	A	Wrong	−1/4
7	E	B	Wrong	−1/4
8	E	C	Wrong	−1/4
9	C	C	Right	+1
10	A	E	Wrong	−1/4
			Total Wrong	−2
			Total Right	+2
			Net Gain	0

In a five-answer multiple-choice item, the chance of getting the item correct by random guessing is 1/5. The chance of getting the item incorrect is 4/5. Therefore, you have a 1/5 chance of getting 1 point and a 4/5 chance of losing 1/4 of a point. Although you gained 2 points for the two correct answers, you lost 2 points for the eight incorrect answers $(8 \times 1/4 = 2)$.

Educated guessing is all about earning a net gain of points on the test. Every time you eliminate even *one* answer choice as being most likely incorrect and guess from what remains, you are nudging your net points higher and higher.

For example, let's say that in ten items, you eliminated two answer choices as wrong for each item. Instead of having a 1-in-5 chance of answering an item correctly, you now have a 1-in-3 chance. Similarly, instead of having a 4-in-5 chance of answering an item incorrectly, you have a 2-in-3 chance. 'What would happen to your net points?

1. Ten items $\times \frac{1}{3}$ chance of guessing correctly $= \frac{10}{3} = 3\frac{1}{3}$ items answered correctly. $3\frac{1}{3}$ items answered correctly $\times$ 1 point for a correct answer $= 3\frac{1}{3}$ points.

2. Ten items $\times \frac{2}{3}$ chance of randomly guessing incorrectly $= \frac{20}{3} = 6\frac{2}{3}$ items answered incorrectly. $6\frac{2}{3} \times -\frac{1}{4}$ points for an incorrect answer $= -1\frac{2}{3}$ points.

3. $3\frac{1}{3}$ points $+ -1\frac{2}{3}$ points $= 1\frac{2}{3}$ net points.

Instead of netting zero points, you've netted almost 2 points—*without knowing the correct answer to any of the ten items.*

As you can see, educated guessing is critical to raising your score. Think of it this way. There are a certain number of items you can answer correctly even if you've never seen the SAT before. That number increases as you become familiar with the test. It increases even more as you use focused test prep materials, such as this *Power Tactics* series.

However, you put a "glass ceiling" on your score potential if you refuse to guess when you've eliminated one or more choices as being most likely incorrect. You must use educated guessing to increase your score.

TACKLING THE ITEMS

Now that you understand how to tackle the test overall, let's focus on each major item type to see what test-taking strategies you should follow on the SAT.

THE MATH SECTION

The Math section tests various concepts in numbers and operations, algebra, geometry, data analysis, statistics, and probability. The first thing you need to do to succeed on the Math section is study up on the concepts that are tested.

Once you've got the basic math down, you'll need a plan to get you through test day. We're going to highlight seven strategies that will help achieve your target score on the Math section.

Plugging in Numbers for Variables

This is a very valuable strategy you can use on the Math section, especially on long, hard-to-follow word problems. Essentially, it turns an algebra item into a simple numbers and operations item by using numbers instead of variables.

We'll use an algebra item to show you how this strategy works:

5. Fred had $3b$ bicycles for sale at a price of d dollars each. If x is the number of bicycles he did NOT sell, which of the following represents the total dollar amount he received in sales from the bicycles?

(A) $(3bx)d$
(B) $(x + 3b)d$
(C) $(3b - x)d$
(D) $(3d - x)b$
(E) $3 + bxd$

Let's assume you can't translate the word problem into a mathematical expression. Choose some numbers for the variables, as follows:

$$b = 2$$

$$d = 4$$

$$x = 3$$

The numbers don't have to be realistic. They just need to be easy to calculate.

Now substitute those numerical values for the variables in the stem—change this item from algebra to a very logical arithmetic problem:

1. Fred has 3(2) bicycles = 6 bicycles total.
2. Each costs $4.
3. He did NOT sell 3 of them.
4. Therefore, he sold 6 − 3 = 3 of them for $4 each.
5. 3 bicycles × $4 per bicycle = $12 received in sales from the bicycles.

Okay, fine, you say. Now what? How does that help me? You know the correct answer choice is going to be the one that spits out 12 when you use $b = 2$, $d = 4$, and $x = 3$. Let's see how it goes. Start with **A**:

A: $(3bx)d = (3 \times 2 \times 3)4 = 72$
Incorrect; eliminate.

B: $(x + 3b)d = (3 + 3 \times 2)4 = 36$
Incorrect; eliminate.

C: $(3b - x)d (3 \times 2 - 3)4 = 12$
Correct.

D: $(3d - x)b = (3 \times 4 - 3)2 = 18$
Incorrect; eliminate.

E: $3 + bxd = 3 + (2 \times 3 \times 4) = 27$
Incorrect; eliminate.

If you are running out of time, after you eliminated **A** and **B**, you can guess from among the other three choices and beat the wrong-answer penalty.

Plugging Numbers from the Answer Choices Back into the Stem

Here's another powerful way to turn algebra into basic math:

2. If $x + 2x = 5x - x + 20$, then $x =$

(A) −20
(B) −10
(C) 5
(D) 10
(E) 20

Let's say you can't do the algebra. No worries. With this method, start with **C**'s value and plug it into the stem's equation. Why start with **C**? Because *SAT answer choices are always listed in numerical order, from largest to smallest or smallest to largest*. You're starting with the middle value. If it doesn't work, you often (but not always) know whether you need a bigger or smaller number—that is, you know whether to go to **B** or to **D** next. Sit tight: this will become clear as we run through the example.

Okay, now we're ready to go:

Choice **C** says $x = 5$. So $x + 2x = 5x - x + 20$ becomes:

$$5 + (2 \times 5) = (5 \times 5) - 5 + 20$$

$$5 + 10 = (25) - 5 + 20$$

$$15 = 40$$

Well, that's not true. Eliminate **C**.

In this example, it's not easy to tell whether you need a bigger or smaller number, so let's try **B**. Don't worry about knowing whether to go up or down with this method. Sometimes it'll be obvious to you. Other times, just choose one or the other. Remember, you can always bail after eliminating even one choice.

Choice **B** says $x = -10$. So $x + 2x = 5x - x + 20$ becomes:

$$-10 + (2 \times -10) = (5 \times -10) - (-10) + 20$$

$$-10 + (-20) = (-50) + 10 + 20$$

$$-30 = -20$$

Well, that's not true, either, so eliminate **B**.

Note that if you are running out of time, you can guess from among the three remaining choices and beat that wrong-answer penalty.

But let's try choice **A**.

Choice **A** says $x = -20$. So $x + 2x = 5x - x + 20$ becomes:

$$-20 + (2 \times -20) = (5 \times -20) - (-20) + 20$$

$$-20 + (-40) = (-100) + 20 + 20$$

$$-60 = -100 + 40$$

$$-60 = -60$$

Bingo. That's a true statement. Choice **A** is correct.

When in Doubt, Draw It Out

Many geometry items will ask you to imagine a figure. Whenever a figure is described but not shown, you should use information in the stem to draw a picture to orient yourself.

When in Doubt, Write It Out

A related point is that you should write out your math work as much as possible. Don't sacrifice accuracy for speed. Particularly on algebra items, writing out each step helps to prevent careless errors.

What Do I Know? Where Do I Need to Go?

In general, when confronted with a Math item, ask yourself these two questions. Let's look at the bicycle item again. What do we know? Where do we need to go?

5. Fred had $3b$ bicycles for sale at a price of d dollars each. If x is the number of bicycles he did NOT sell, which of the following represents the total dollar amount he received in sales from the bicycles?

What do we know?

- Fred had a certain number of bikes he was selling.
- He was selling them at a certain price in dollars.
- He *didn't* sell all of his bikes.

Where do we need to go?

- Some algebraic expression that tells us how much he made, in dollars, from the bikes he *did* sell.

Asking these two questions separates the known from the unknown, which is, after all, a large part of mathematical reasoning, especially in algebra. It focuses your attention on what steps you'll need to take to get from the known to the unknown, which is especially helpful for multi-step, complex items.

Calculators

The best advice is: *use your calculator rarely.* If you could answer every item on the SAT by just plugging numbers into your calculator, you wouldn't be allowed to have a calculator during testing. The fact that you're allowed to have a calculator on the test day tells you two things:

1. This is not a test that's designed to assess your ability to calculate directly—especially because anyone can buy a calculator or use a computer in the real world.
2. If you see a way to solve an item that requires heavy calculations, you're probably missing the point. Don't run to your calculator just because you have a little machine to lean on. *Think* before you start hitting buttons.

Usually, your calculator will come in handy to solve a step in your solution to an item. But overall, you'll have to use your brain to do most of the reasoning.

Grid-Ins

Because grid-ins don't include answer choices, you won't be able to plug in numbers as easily. Furthermore, you won't be able to make an educated guess because there are no answers to eliminate. The good news is that there is no wrong-answer penalty on grid-ins. Always put *something* down, even if you're not certain it is the correct answer. If worse comes to worst, you will get zero points for that item.

If you follow a few simple rules with grid-ins, you'll never mess up on this section. Grid-ins:

- Can't have negative answers. If you get a negative answer, you made a mistake.

- Can have more than one correct answer. If you find two or more answers for the item, pick one and move on.
- Cannot accommodate mixed numbers. The scanning machine reads $2\frac{3}{4}$ as $\frac{23}{4}$, so change your mixed numbers into either proper fractions or decimals.
- Cannot accommodate a zero before a decimal point, so instead of gridding in 0.34, grid in .34.

With decimals—especially repeating decimals—don't round up. Just start with the leftmost bubble and fill in all four spaces. You'll never be penalized for not rounding up but you might be penalized for rounding up inappropriately.

THE WRITING AND CRITICAL READING SECTIONS

One key point to remember is how intertwined the skills these section tests are. Each piece of the Writing and Critical Reading sections looks at language from a different angle, but essentially what's being tested is your proficiency in good writing and the English language as a whole. Studying for one section will help you prepare for the others.

Multiple-Choice Writing

Bombing Runs are especially important on the Writing section. Always do Identifying Sentence Errors first, then Improving Sentences, and finally Improving Paragraphs. Within each item type, fly Bombing Runs to distribute your knowledge as efficiently as possible. Remember, unlike Sentence Completions on the Critical Reading section, the multiple-choice items on the Writing section are not listed by order of difficulty.

The Essay

The biggest mistake you can make on the essay is to start writing without planning what you're going to write. You have a very short amount of time (25 minutes) to construct a well-organized, well-written argument. Even though the essay is meant to be a first draft, your essay needs to show your ability to think critically and write accurately and forcefully.

Everything you do for the essay should flow from the **scoring rubric**—the grading criteria used by essay readers. The scoring rubric doesn't emphasize the *content* of your essay (for example, quoting Dante rather than relating an anecdote from your life) but rather the *structure* of your argument and the *clarity* of your writing.

Despite what you might think or may have been told, writing—even timed SAT essay writing—is as learnable a skill as any other—it's not magic. To succeed on the essay, make sure you read the prompt carefully and plan a structure for your essay before you actually start writing. This process will take only a few minutes and will go a long way toward improving your score.

Reading Passages

The key is not to read long passages word for word. It's a waste of time—time you'll need for the items themselves. You need to know what to read and what to skim in the long passages. Then you need to fly Bombing Runs among the items in the set.

Skimming is pretty simple. Instead of reading the entire passage word for word, you want to get a general idea of what the passage discusses. Here's how you do it:

- **Read only the first and last sentences in paragraphs.**
- **Circle or underline signpost words or key terms.** Terms deemed as key will vary from reader to reader, but the idea is to identify some important terms, as well as those important signpost words.
- **Use your pencil to help you break the habit of reading every word.** Move the tip of your pencil across the lines of text quickly enough to make it impossible for you to read every word. This forces you to skip over some words and phrases, which means you are actually *skimming*.

Bombing runs at the section level are more complex, as we alluded to earlier. We discuss Sentence Completions in the next section, but assuming those are done, you need to decide which of the Reading Passages, if there is more than one, you should attack first.

In general, hit the short passages first. They are a lower investment and yield the same number of points for each item. Decide which to hit first based on subject matter and/or length. If the choice is between two long passages, again, subject matter and length should determine which set you'll hit first. Treat paired passages as separate long passages: read/skim passage 1 and do those items first, then read/skim passage 2 and do those items, and finally work on the hardest items—the compare-and-contrast items based on both passages.

Sentence Completions

The key to Sentence Completions is to have some idea of the answer before you look at the answer choices. Fortunately, because Sentence Completions test your reading skills at the sentence level, the structure of the sentence stem often helps you generate a likely answer. Sentence Completions test vocabulary *in context*. If you understand the sentence in the stem, you'll be able to come up with your own answers for the blanks.

STUDYING FOR THE SAT

Strategies for taking the test are only one part of the equation. You also need to approach your *preparation* for the test strategically.

This section gives you advice on how to maximize your studying and preparation for the SAT.

ESTABLISH A BASELINE SCORE

The first thing you need to do is take a full-length diagnostic test in the most testlike conditions possible. Taking a real SAT test before you begin your studying will pinpoint your strengths and weaknesses. Log onto SparkNotes' test prep site at **testprep.sparknotes.com** to take a free practice test. The score you receive on this test will be your baseline score. This score tells you how well you would score on the SAT without any practice or preparation.

The advantage to using our online test is that you receive instant scoring and feedback. The feedback tells you what sections and item types you need to focus on in preparing for the exam. If you score well on geometry, you know you don't need to spend too much time preparing for those items. The extra time you save on those items can go toward preparing for a section you're having more trouble with. If you score poorly on Reading Passages, you can focus your study and preparation on that part of the test.

ESTABLISH A TARGET SCORE

There are several factors that determine what score you'd like to achieve:

- What your baseline score is. If you score low, aim for the middle range. If you score in the middle range, aim a bit higher.
- The amount of time you have to study before the test.

- The average scores of the most recent freshman class at the schools you want to attend. This information is usually available from the schools' admissions offices.
- What else you need to do between now and test day. Remember, the SAT is one piece of the admissions pie. Don't overprepare for that one piece if it means slacking off on your grades, application essays, or extracurricular activities.

Your target score should not be 2400—even if you have a realistic shot at that. The idea is to use your baseline scores to identify weaknesses and to determine what you need to spend the most time on as you study. Try to get away from the number. Focusing on a set number, especially an unrealistic target score, is counterproductive. We'll return to this point when we discuss test anxiety.

ESTABLISH A STUDY PLAN

Like anything else that requires practice, preparing for the SAT works better when you spread it out over time. Don't cram in all your prep time at once. Studying for ten hours in one day is much less productive than spreading those ten hours over a week. Set up a schedule that ensures you do a little SAT work every day. Try to do at least half an hour a day and try to avoid more than two hours a day.

Use your baseline scores to balance the time you'll spend on each portion of the test. If you have a couple of months or more before test day, start with your weaknesses. If you have less than a month, start with your strengths to make sure you hone those, then jump to weaknesses with plenty of time to get up to speed as much as you can. These time management decisions depend on a number of other factors, as we've discussed (e.g., your coursework), but you shouldn't have too much trouble working up a study plan.

We suggest using a wall calendar for SAT prep. Make sure to build in full-length practice tests periodically so you can gauge your progress, build up your endurance, and even alter your study plan as you progress.

The key thing is to work your schedule *backward* from the application due dates for all the schools to which you're applying. This way, your SAT prep is somewhat related to your school-selection process—the due dates factor into which test date you select. Leave one last-chance date open that will still get to your schools on time in case you're not happy with your score. The average SAT scores of schools, along with a host of other factors, play a role in which schools you'll select.

ESTABLISH A STUDY SPACE

This really matters. You need a quiet place free from distractions. It may be your home, but you may find all the comforts of home—TV, stereo, video games—distracting when you sit down to study. If that's the case, work at your local or school library, or find a coffee shop you like. You know yourself best. Put yourself in a situation in which you're most likely to focus.

BUILD YOUR VOCABULARY

Building your vocabulary will help maximize your score on the Critical Reading and Writing sections. Although the SAT will never ask you to define a word, it will ask you to explain what a word means in context. Often you can figure out this meaning without actually knowing what a word means, but on harder items, the context might not be enough to guide you to an answer.

When you come across a word whose meaning you don't know, write it down and look up the definition. Once you have your words and definitions on hand, create **flashcards** by writing the word on one side and the definition on the other. You should also create groupings for your flashcards, such as positive words, negative words, words of praise, and so forth. Finally, create a sample sentence that uses the word. Here's what your flashcards should look like:

ubiquity

Noun. A presence that is everywhere or in most places simultaneously; omnipresence.

The ring of the cell phone is a ubiquity in contemporary life.

Grouping: Presence/Absence
ubiquitous

READ

Reading a little every day not only helps build your vocabulary but also hones your critical thinking skills. It gives you excellent preparation for the type of Reading Passages you'll see and allows you to practice the kind of active reading you need for the SAT. Furthermore, even though your essay is intended to be a first draft, one of the best ways to improve your writing is to read the works of excellent writers.

Read conventional, nonexperimental fiction from the last 100 years or so, as well as nonfiction from newspapers and magazines, such as the *The New York Times*, *Harper's*, *National Geographic*, *Smithsonian*, *Scientific American*, *The Nation*, *The Economist*, *The Wall Street Journal*, and *Atlantic*. You can find these periodicals in your local library. Many of these publications also have free online versions. This is by no means an exhaustive list, but we purposely chose only very well-written magazines and newspapers.

If you're looking for some fiction to read, stick with the more conventional authors—folks you'd read in school, most likely, such as John Steinbeck, Ernest Hemingway, George Orwell, and Toni Morrison.

DO YOUR COURSEWORK

Part of your daily reading will come out of your English coursework. However, remember that passages are taken from all areas of fiction, science, history, art, and architecture. So pay close attention to your textbooks and the other reading material you're given.

Concentrate on planning out your papers for school. Plan what your arguments are first, then write them down. The SAT essay is designed to weed out those who simply start writing without having first thought through the issue at hand.

In your math classes, use your SAT prep to nail down concepts that have always given you trouble (what the heck *is* the Triangle Inequality Theorem, anyway?), and pay special attention to second-year algebra, because some of those concepts will be on the new SAT.

TACKLING TEST ANXIETY

The most common barrier to achieving your maximum score on the SAT is anxiety about the test. Anxiety is as real a thing as the pain you feel when you stub your toe. The good news is there are tried-and-true ways of reducing anxiety. Here's a plan you should follow that will lead you right up to test day.

MONTHS BEFORE THE TEST

"This Test Sucks"

The SAT looms so large that students are often aware of it in elementary school. Even though we struggle to keep students, teachers, and colleges from concentrating too much on this one score, the process of shedding our culture's hysteria about the SAT is challenging. So the first thing you need to do is tune out all this noise about the test. The SAT is just one part of your application to college. It's designed to predict how well you'll do in your first semester of college. That's it. That's all it's meant to do.

Students often approach the SAT by saying "It's all bull" or "It's stupid" or "I'm not good at these kinds of tests." Regardless of whether these points are valid, don't let your distaste for the test prevent you from doing as well as you can. When all is said and done, you still have to take the test. Do the best you can, go to college, and change the world from there. Go ahead and complain about it every so often, but don't let your criticism of the SAT become an excuse not to prepare. It's not going away any time soon.

Take Control and Get Started

Sometimes the anxiety around the SAT is so intense that students have trouble starting their preparation for the test. They end up procrastinat ing, which means they have less time to prepare, which in turn leads to more anxiety.

Don't fall into this cycle. Take control of your test prep experience by taking a full-length practice test and establishing a baseline score. Once you have this score on hand, you'll be able to shape the rest of your studying and preparation by focusing on your weaknesses and determining a realistic target score. You will then be able to set up a study schedule that will get you where you need to be by test day.

Conquering your fear of starting the process might be the biggest challenge to overcome. Beginning things is often as hard as finishing them. Once you're rolling, huge, daunting tasks are suddenly broken down into smaller, doable tasks. Your sense of control rises, and your anxiety starts to slip away.

So take control. Get a baseline score, set up your study schedule and space, gather your materials, and dive right in. Work, which is something we all like to avoid at one point or another, is an excellent antidote to fear.

A MONTH BEFORE THE TEST

By this point, you have spent time building up the concepts you need, absorbing and practicing the strategies to use, and doing your outside reading, vocabulary building, and coursework. Now is the time to start timing yourself on practice sets. You should be familiar enough with the test and your abilities on each section to begin placing yourself in testlike conditions.

If you're using one of the other books in this *Power Tactics* series, take the online posttests to see how much progress you've made since you established your baseline score. Also get your hands on some additional real SATs and take them one section at a time to hone your set- and section-level Bombing Run capabilities.

Make sure to take at least one full-length test in a timed, testlike situation—especially if you haven't taken one since the initial one you took to get your baseline score. Also make sure to compose at least one essay in a timed, testlike situation. You can find several prompts in the essay book in this series.

Begin getting up early on weekends if you don't normally do so. Get your body in that habit—it helps. As far as specific foods go, the simple truth of nutrition is to eat balanced meals. Don't alter your food intake radically unless you eat only junk food. Get your gut used to a nutritious morning meal.

A WEEK BEFORE THE TEST

Take a full-length test in a timed, testlike situation, including the essay. Review your books, notes, and explanations to practice items. Work on some final vocabulary building. But generally, take it easy. Resist the urge to overstudy, which will inevitably cause needless anxiety. You've put in the effort and proven it to yourself through steady progress. Trust that effort. It will pay off.

We talked about registering for the test earlier. If your test site isn't at a familiar location, take a drive in the morning to see how to get there and how much traffic there is. Don't leave finding the site to the day of the test. Who needs that kind of pressure?

THE DAY BEFORE THE TEST

Our advice for the day before the test is:

- Don't do *any* SAT prep work!
- Don't do *any* SAT prep work!
- Don't do *any* SAT prep work!

Whatever factoid you might gain the night before will be more than outweighed by the anxiety you'll be producing. Watch a movie. Hang out with friends. Read a book. Play a video game. Go for a run. Do something other than studying for the SAT.

Run through the following checklist and put everything in your bag or backpack the night before so you won't have to worry about it in the morning:

Timepiece	
Approved calculator with fresh batteries	
Approved backup calculator with fresh batteries	
More fresh batteries	
At least four sharpened No. 2 pencils	
A small pencil sharpener	
An extra big eraser that really works	
A photo ID	

Your admissions ticket	
A snack	
Tissues, even if you're not sniffly	
Layers, in case it's cold in the room	
A portable CD or mp3 player, if you think music will calm or focus you during breaks	

Remember:

- You can't use an alarm during the test.
- You can't eat or drink during the test inside the testing room.
- You can't bring in any scratch paper, notes, books, highlighters, pens, protractors, etc. Check out the full list of accepted and prohibited materials at: **http://www.collegeboard.com/student/testing/sat/testday/bring.html**
- You can't use your mp3 player or CD player inside the test room.
- You must turn off your cell phone.

Go to bed at your usual time. If you can't fall asleep, don't worry about it. Worrying is what keeps you awake. Try some deep-breathing exercises and realize that no matter how little sleep you end up getting, you'll be revved up for the test, come morning.

TEST DAY

Here's what you need to do:

- Wake up early enough to eat your normal nutritious breakfast and relax. You should be able to go through your usual routine without feeling rushed but with still enough time to get to the test site at least 30 minutes early. You'll want to avoid, if possible, the unforeseen disasters of traffic or other wacky delays.
- Do not drink a lot of caffeine. Drink whatever amount you're used to, if you drink any at all. Caffeine is a diuretic—you don't want to need bathroom breaks or to feel distracted by having to go and not wanting to take a break.
- Grab your prepacked bag and go.
- Once you arrive at the test site, be selfish. Do whatever you need to do to put yourself in the proper mindset. Talk to friends, listen to music, be by yourself. Do whatever relaxes you.

- When the test starts, stay calm. Trust your preparation and effort. It will pay off. Focus completely on the test. Drown out all other sensory input, aside from your timepiece. Don't even think about how you're doing or scoring—just do it. You are an efficient, savvy, test-taking machine. Take control of that test.

WORST-CASE SCENARIOS

We hope everything will run smoothly on test day. On the off chance that something does go wrong, keep in mind that there is always a solution.

Scenario 1: Your test booklet is blank, missing pages, or pages are stuck together.

Don't panic. Just raise your hand and the proctor will handle it.

Scenario 2: Your neighbor is coughing or fidgeting.

Don't be polite. Raise your hand and have the proctor move you.

Scenario 3: Your calculator stops working.

Always bring extra batteries and a backup calculator with you. If your backup breaks too—well, the odds are pretty slim, and even if it does, you *rarely* need to use your calculator on the test.

Scenario 4: You freeze or have an anxiety or panic attack.

Take a minute or two to do the following:

- Stop what you're doing.
- Look up from the test and out a window, if possible, or at a poster or blackboard. Focus on that completely. Alternatively, close your eyes and picture a beautiful, calm place you've been to or even just imagined. Force yourself to breathe deeply, slowly, and rhythmically.
- Stretch your arms and back to loosen up any tension.
- Return to what you were doing.

Scenario 5: You misgrid your answers.

Raise your hand and talk to the proctor about it. You may or may not be allowed to regrid your test, so be careful when filling in those tiny bubbles.

Unless something completely wacky occurs—such as you have mono when you take the test, the power goes out, or you totally misgrid or omit an entire section—resist the temptation to cancel your score. Most people underestimate how well they've done, and after almost four hours of high-level, adrenaline-fueled concentration, you'll be crashing. Most likely, canceling your score is a bad idea.

You're allowed until the Wednesday following your test date to cancel your score. Your biochemistry should be stable by then, but still think long and hard about canceling what may be a great score.

EMERGENCY STUDY PLANS

What If I Have Only a Month to Prepare?

Don't panic. First ask yourself whether you have to take the test right now. If this is your last chance to take the SAT before your application deadlines, you'll have to bear down. Here's a good mantra for you: *it is what it is*. Deal with it—you actually have less time for the luxury of anxiety.

First take a full-length test in testlike conditions to generate a baseline score. Then spend more time honing your strengths than trying to boost your weaknesses. Concentrate on thinking strategically about your study plan. Here's an extended example of what we mean:

You take a full-length test and get a 620 on Math, a 480 on Critical Reading, and a 550 on Writing. Be strategic about investing your time on the most high-yield areas. Basically, you're flying a Bombing Run on your *study time*. Study how you did in Math. You're scoring well. Is there a discrete concept or set of concepts you're missing out on, for example, functions? If so, master that. You'll raise your score with little effort.

Do the same kind of thinking for the other two sections. What's the least time-consuming, simplest item type in Critical Reading? Sentence Completions. Focus on those first, followed by Short Reading Passages, then Long Reading Passages. With so little time left to prepare, you are better off acing Sentence Completions first, then turning to Reading Passages if you have time.

For Writing, don't even worry about Improving Paragraphs. It's the highest investment item type. Concentrate on the sentence-level items:

Identifying Sentence Errors and Improving Sentences. As far as the Essay goes, concentrate on organizing and planning for a few minutes before writing. That will almost certainly raise your score.

You also want to focus on the basic test-taking strategies. Learn how to fly Bombing Runs and use the wrong-answer penalty to your advantage. Remember, you don't necessarily need to know the correct answer to answer it.

Finally, take a full-length test the week before test day.

What If I Have Only a Week to Prepare?

Do you *really* have to take the test? If the answer isn't "Yes, absolutely! This is my last chance!" then put it off.

However, if you're stuck, basically follow an accelerated version of the plan outlined above, but spend even more time on honing strategies, especially Bombing Runs, to maximize the knowledge you already have. You'll get a much bigger bang for your buck by mastering test-taking strategies at this point than by spending a day learning all about triangles.

So take a practice full-length test to get a baseline score, analyze it, and spend your week tackling the test-taking strategies in this book. Take another full-length test two days before test day.

Even though you're cramming, we don't suggest you do much the day before. Anxiety will probably be running high—whatever concepts you shove into your head 24 hours before the test most likely won't do you much good.

No time for panic. Buckle down, maintain your sleep and exercise, and maximize your score in the brief time you have.

CONGRATULATIONS

You've done a lot to prepare—just trust that preparation and let the day progress. Tackle your test as best you can. Then go home and don't think about it.

AFTER TEST DAY

Let's begin with the second you hand in your bubble sheet and walk out of the test room.

AFTER YOU HAND IN YOUR SHEET

As they say in New York City, "Fuhgeddaboudit!" (That's "forget about it," by the way.) It's done. Have fun for the rest of the day. At least give yourself some time to chill out. Don't think about the score. Don't replay the game in your head. You'll get the "tape" soon enough.

GETTING YOUR SCORE

You'll automatically receive your score report by mail within about three weeks. For the patience-challenged, you can phone The College Board or log onto its Web site to get your score about eight days before they get mailed. There's a fee for the phone service. Viewing scores online is free.

WHAT TO DO WITH YOUR SCORE

If you matched or exceeded your target score, great. Congratulations!

If you didn't match it, consider whether you should take the test again. We discussed that decision earlier in this book. It all depends on how schools deal with multiple scores and several other factors. Definitely compare your score with your prospective schools' score ranges from the previous year's freshman class. Discuss it with your teachers, parents, and guidance counselor. Don't just automatically reregister.

If you decide to take the test again, study your score report in detail, item by item. See where you went wrong. Were you running out of time at the end of sections? Did you not bail out often enough? Did you not fly Bombing Runs enough? Were you careless or overconfident?

In other words, don't fret—*diagnose*. Then reregister, study up again, concentrating on whatever you need to raise your score and achieve your potential.

IF YOU'RE SATISFIED, MOVE ON

Work on your applications. Keep your grades up. Look into whether your prospective schools require SAT IIs, and if so, which ones. Look into taking AP tests. Of course, you've been doing some of this planning all along, but a big task is now off your plate. Enjoy that fact. You've earned it.

THE 15 MOST COMMON MISTAKES

As you prepare for the new SAT, keep the following common mistakes in mind. Some are mistakes to avoid when taking the actual test. Others are mistakes to avoid during your preparation for the test.

1. Looking at the answer choices without having some idea of what the correct answer should be.
2. Spending more than a minute or so on any one item in a set.
3. Failing to practice sufficiently—*reading* this book is not enough!
4. Refusing to guess when you've eliminated one answer choice.
5. Trying to manipulate equations in your head instead of writing it down and solving it.
6. Not picking the answer the item asks for. Often this is not the same thing as finding the critical value needed to solve the item.
7. Answering every item in order.
8. Rushing through a set instead of thinking each item through.
9. Refusing to fly Bombing Runs—that is, not doing items out of order based on your assessment of which will be easiest.
10. Not establishing a baseline score.
11. Setting an unrealistic target score.
12. Not building up your vocabulary.
13. Not creating a study plan.
14. Not taking a full-length practice test before test day.
15. Doing SAT prep work the day before the test.

CONCLUSION

Remember, the key goal for the SAT is to maximize your potential. Resist the temptation to compete with others on this issue. At worst, it will jack up your anxiety level. At best, it might let you blow off steam by competing with others on practice test scores and total hours studied and whatnot, but you're very likely causing a spike in someone else's anxiety level, whether they show it or not.

The SAT is merely one of those hurdles in life we all have to jump over. It might be right, it might be wrong—like most things in life, it's somewhere in between—but the point is that you have this task, right or wrong, in front of you. Adopt a positive attitude to clear your mind of all the understandable worries and concerns you have. Take control. Free your mind up for *learning*. You will actually learn some useful things as you prepare for this test.

Finally, the SAT is just one part of your entire application package. Preparing efficiently willfree up time you need to maintain or improve your grades, to study for other standardized tests you might take, to continue your extracurricular activities, and to prepare your application essay.

THE PRACTICE SETS

BOMBING RUN PRACTICE SETS

As we've emphasized, one of the most important test-taking strategies is flying Bombing Runs. You need to determine which items in a set are most likely going to be the easiest for you and which to put off until later.

In the following section, you'll find three sets:

- Set 1: Sentence Completions from a Critical Reading section.
- Set 2: Multiple choice from a Math section.
- Set 3: Identifying Sentence Errors from a Writing section.

For each set, read all the *stems* and determine in which order to attempt the items. You can write down the order in the margins or on a separate piece of paper. If you've already studied these item types, go ahead and complete the sets. This second step is less important. Here, we just want you to focus on practicing Bombing Runs.

When you're done, turn the page to see in what order we chose to attack these items. Realize that these decisions are personal, so don't fret if your order doesn't exactly match ours. *Your* strengths are what determine how you'll fly Bombing Runs.

So get cracking on your SAT preparation. We wish you the best of luck on your test and in all that you do.

PRACTICE SET 1: SENTENCE COMPLETIONS

Read through the items and choose the order in which to attempt them. When you're done, compare your decision-making process with ours.

1. Drinking one alcoholic drink per day is strongly ___ by many doctors for its health benefits.

    (A) advocated
    (B) dictated
    (C) forbidden
    (D) disallowed
    (E) banned

2. At first, the stylish boutique was a ___ success, with hundreds of customers jamming its aisles each day; however, after its initially low prices rose, its popularity plummeted.

    (A) marginal
    (B) moderate
    (C) modest
    (D) massive
    (E) reasonable

3. Lucy often blames her lack of friends on her ___, although she is not particularly introverted.

    (A) comeliness
    (B) timidity
    (C) extroversion
    (D) hostility
    (E) garrulousness

4. Rita was obviously ___ about her boyfriend's behavior: she shredded his picture into tiny pieces.

    (A) incensed
    (B) apprehensive
    (C) apathetic
    (D) ignorant
    (E) sentimental

5. Nat King Cole was a ___ jazz singer whose voice still echoes on the radio today; interestingly, he always ___ the many cigarettes he smoked each day as his secret to his vocal prowess.

    (A) mediocre . . . hailed
    (B) phenomenal . . . credited
    (C) competent . . . praised
    (D) groveling . . . lauded
    (E) liminal . . . extolled

6. Aspirin has recently been lauded as a ___; many experts believe that it can ___ all sorts of illness.

    (A) blight . . . exacerbate
    (B) plague . . . exaggerate
    (C) panacea . . . alleviate
    (D) cure-all . . . induce
    (E) pandemic . . . assuage

7. A job in which one is paid solely on commissions can often be ___ because income is never guaranteed.

    (A) tenuous
    (B) consoling
    (C) opportune
    (D) rigid
    (E) astounding

8. Lorna always thought that raising one child would be ___ because her own mother had raised six children with seemingly no exertion; however, she told me that it is the most ___ task she has ever attempted.

    (A) difficult . . . feasible
    (B) effortless . . . challenging
    (C) leisurely . . . eccentric
    (D) laborious . . . perplexing
    (E) harrowing . . . complex

9. Carlos always chooses the most ___ Halloween costume each year, always sporting severed limbs, fake blood, or other ___ accessories.

   (A) benign ... comely
   (B) macabre ... gory
   (C) ostentatious ... radiant
   (D) ghastly ... celestial
   (E) interesting ... naïve

10. Although the speaker's ideas were not ___, he could not seem to organize them and was described by many listeners as ___.

   (A) intriguing ... discombobulated
   (B) vapid ... muddled
   (C) pedantic ... loquacious
   (D) base ... glib
   (E) spirited ... voluble

EXPLANATIONS

As we've already mentioned, you should attempt all the Sentence Completions you can *before* attacking the Reading Passages. Because Sentence Completions have no passages, they are the lowest investment items in the section. Do them first.

Remember—Sentence Completions go in order of difficulty, from a statistical standpoint. *Your* determination of order of difficulty may or may not match the collected data from hundreds of thousands of test-takers. All that matters is what you think is difficult or easy. By definition, Bombing Runs are personal and based on one's own self-knowledge of skill mastery, which comes from a lot of practice. What we've done is create a particular student's approach. Under the *Why* column, you'll see this student's rationale.

The idea is not to compare the exact order of this fictional student's Bombing Run with your own but rather to compare your *decision-making process* with that of our fictional student, who is flying Bombing Runs correctly, in that she is making decisions on which items to attempt first, based on known skill levels.

Item	Order	Why
1	1st	This is a one-blank Sentence Completion in a straightforward sentence with no twists. A quick scan of the answer choices—and the knowledge that Sentence Completions are in (statistical) order of difficulty—encourages me to think this'll be relatively easily answered.
2	6th	The next-shortest two-blank sentence. The *however* clues me into the type of twist in the sentence I feel comfortable figuring out. (See item 3, which I attempted second.)
3	2nd	This Sentence Completion has one blank. It has a twist—*although*—which means the blank should be something that is the opposite of *introverted*. I'm comfortable with this common subtype.
4	3rd	Another one-blank, which tends to have easier vocabulary. The colon clues me in to the flow of the sentence too. I'll try this one.
5	8th	A long two-blank Sentence Completion, but it doesn't seem to have any logical twists to it.
6	5th	At this point, I've exhausted all the one-blank Sentence Completions. Two-blank Sentence Completions are tough for me—they often require a lot of logical work to figure out what's going on. So I'm starting with the shortest one. A good investment strategy.
7	4th	I happen to know what *commissions* means, so I can handle this late-set one-blank Sentence Completion.
8	9th	Long. Two blanks. I'll try to piece it together if I have time.
9	7th	Two blanks but a straightforward sentence. No confusing twists to puzzle over.
10	10th	This sentence will take some time to figure out. Hard vocabulary in the answer choices. I'll attempt it if I have time.

Answers

1. **A**

2. **D**

3. **B**

4. **A**

5. **B**

6. **C**

7. **A**

8. **B**

9. **B**

10. **B**

PRACTICE SET 2: MULTIPLE-CHOICE MATH

Read through the items and choose the order in which you'll attempt them.
When you're done, compare your decision-making process with ours.

1. If $a^2b = 1$, then $3a^4b^2 =$

    (A) 1
    (B) 1.73
    (C) 2
    (D) 3
    (E) 6

2. What is the midpoint of the line segment described by (1, 4) and (3, 7)?

    (A) (3, 4)
    (B) (1, 7)
    (C) (4, 11)
    (D) (2, 5.5)
    (E) (2, 6.2)

3. Angles a and c are supplementary angles. What is $2 \times (a + c)$?

    (A) 180°
    (B) 360°
    (C) 420°
    (D) 540°
    (E) 600°

4. What fraction of 45 is 60% of 50?

    (A) $\frac{1}{5}$

    (B) $\frac{2}{5}$

(C) $\frac{1}{2}$

(D) $\frac{2}{3}$

(E) $\frac{3}{4}$

5. Two six-sided dice are rolled, one after the other. The first roll shows an odd number. What is the probability that the second die shows an odd number?

(A) $\frac{1}{6}$

(B) $\frac{1}{3}$

(C) $\frac{1}{2}$

(D) $\frac{2}{3}$

(E) 1

6. If $x^2 = -1$ and $[(x^2)^5]^y = -1$, then the least positive integer value of y is

(A) 1
(B) 2
(C) 3
(D) 5
(E) 7

7. Suppose set $S = \{2, 4, 4, 6, 7, 13\}$. Which of the following statements are true of S?

      I.   The mean of S is 6.
      II.   The median of S is greater than the mode of S.
      III.   The mean and mode of S are elements of S.

(A) I only
(B) II only
(C) I and II only
(D) I and III only
(E) I, II, and III

8. Seth works at a museum for $8 an hour and makes $256 a week. He is given a 20% raise. Assuming he works the same number of hours per day, how much more money does he make a week after getting a raise?

   (A) $21.00
   (B) $36.40
   (C) $51.20
   (D) $64.30
   (E) $88.90

9. If the equation of a line is $y = 2x + 9$, what is the equation of the line perpendicular to it that has a y-intercept of 10?

   (A) $y = 2x - 9$

   (B) $y = 2x - \dfrac{1}{9}$

   (C) $y = \dfrac{1}{2}x + 10$

   (D) $y = -\dfrac{1}{2}x + 10$

   (E) $y = -\dfrac{1}{2}x - 10$

10. If $x^{-2} = 25$, what is the value of $\left(\dfrac{25}{x}\right)^{\frac{1}{3}}$?

    (A) 0
    (B) 5
    (C) 15
    (D) 25
    (E) 125

EXPLANATIONS

The key decisions on the Math sections revolve around **content area**: numbers & operations, algebra, geometry, and so forth. Decisions may be refined to **subareas**: for example, triangle problems versus circle problems. Also, you may want to put off some or all of the word problems until last and do all the simple calculation items first.

As you practice, you get a good sense of what you should attempt first and what you should leave for last.

Item	Order	Why
1	8th	I'm not a fan of algebra. I can't really work backward on this one, but it's first in the set, so there should be some key concept that makes it easy. I'll try to work it out.
2	1st	I'm good at geometry. I know this formula cold. I'm going to snag this point right now.
3	2nd	I know this fact too. I'm going to grab this point.
4	6th	Looked complicated at first glance, but now that I've gotten five items under my belt, I'm going to try to work this one out. I'm pretty good at arithmetic. I just need to take it step by step and be careful.
5	5th	I tend to leave word problems for later in the set, unless they're clearly geometrical problems. Anyway, I think I know what they're getting at here, so I'll try this one now.
6	9th	Only if I have time. All those nested parentheses. There has to be a shortcut of some kind.
7	4th	Mean, median, and mode are pretty familiar to me. Also, I know I can eliminate answer choices in roman numeral questions as I disprove statements. This won't take too long.
8	7th	Arithmetical word problem. Time to attempt this one.
9	3rd	This one might be tough for many, but I know my geometry cold. I've got this fact at my fingertips, so I'll grab this point.
10	10th	Huh? I heard negative and fractional exponents would be on the test, but I never really got that straight. I may actually not even attempt this one at all. If I have time, I'll see if I can get anywhere, but a random guess is not a good idea.

Answers

1. **D**

2. **D**

3. **B**

4. **D**

5. **C**

6. **A**

7. **C**

8. **C**

9. **D**

10. **D**

PRACTICE SET 3: IDENTIFYING SENTENCE ERRORS

Read through the items and choose the order in which to attempt them. When you're done, compare your decision making process to ours.

1. <u>The teachers</u> did not expect a complete victory, but they had
        A

    <u>counted on</u> <u>the university</u> granting at least some of <u>his or her</u>
        B   C   D

    main requests. <u>No error</u>
                   E

2. <u>Strewn around</u> his <u>playpen was</u> the <u>toddler's</u> favorite toys,
        A   B   C

    including a miniature car and <u>a set of</u> alphabet blocks. <u>No error</u>
                                        D   E

3. If you are going to Beijing in December, it is essential <u>to dress</u> in
                                                       A

    layers, <u>as</u> the sudden changes of temperature <u>there</u> can
            B   C

    <u>catch one</u>off guard. <u>No error</u>
       D   E

4. At the school assembly, one candidate for student council made

    a speech <u>where</u> <u>he</u> proposed <u>holding</u> a blood drive <u>in the fall.</u>
             A   B   C   D

    <u>No error</u>
     E

5. More <u>devotedly</u> <u>as any</u> nun in the church, Mother Teresa worked
         A   B

    <u>long hours</u> to restore the health of the patients <u>in her hospital.</u>
      C   D

    <u>No error</u>
     E

6. The typical American high school student has to <u>take out</u>
    _A
    several loans <u>in order to</u> attend college because <u>in the last</u> thirty
    _B   _C
    years <u>they have</u> grown extremely expensive. <u>No error</u>
    _D   _E

7. The governor, as well as all fifty members <u>of his staff,</u> <u>have been</u>
    _A   _B
    working <u>nonstop</u> on the <u>reelection</u> campaign. <u>No error.</u>
    _C   _D   _E

8. The student declared that he could <u>not scarcely</u> imagine a better
    _A
    <u>role model</u> for Sarah Lawrence students <u>than</u> Alice Walker,
    _B   _C
    <u>herself</u> a Sarah Lawrence alumna. <u>No error</u>
    _D   _E

9. The month of July <u>has</u> so long <u>been associated</u> with vacations
    _A   _B
    that <u>the very mention</u> of the month conjures up visions of
    _C
    barbecues, fireworks, and <u>the beach.</u> <u>No error</u>
    _D   _E

10. The guest lecturer <u>strode up</u> to the podium, put down his
    _A
    papers, <u>and without</u> introduction <u>began</u> to read <u>from it.</u> <u>No error</u>
    _B   _C   _D   _E

EXPLANATIONS

Remember to attack all Writing *sections* in the following order:

1. Do the Identifying Sentence Errors first. Lowest investment, same point yield.
2. Do the Improving Sentences next. Next lowest investment, same point yield.
3. Finally, if you have time, attempt the Improving Paragraphs. Highest investment—there's a passage to absorb—same point yield.

In the special case of Identifying Sentence Errors, reading the stem means reading the answer choices too—they're embedded in the stem. This format means that you'll probably complete items as you read them. Otherwise, you'll save them for last (which is what we did with items 2,

4, and 9). So read this chart a bit differently. Read the *Why* column from top to bottom. Check out the order after you've read the rationales.

Item	Order	Why
1	1st	I'm good on agreement. *The teachers . . . his or her?* No good.
2	8th	Not immediately obvious to me. I'll skip this one for now.
3	2nd	I see this one immediately. I'll grab this point. The key is to move fast in Multiple-Choice Writing.
4	9th	Hmmmm . . . not sure. Move on.
5	3rd	Idiomatically incorrect. Nail it, move on.
6	4th	Whoops—agreement issue again. I got this one.
7	5th	Agreement again.
8	6th	Ah, a classic incorrect idiom—the double negative. Got this one.
9	10th	Not sure. Let's see about item 10.
10	7th	Another agreement one. Got it. Let's go back, if I have time.

Answers

1. **D**

2. **B**

3. **D**

4. **A**

5. **B**

6. **D**

7. **B**

8. **A**

9. **E**

10. **D**

ABOUT THE AUTHOR

Doug Tarnopol brings a unique mix of talents and experience to SparkNotes and *Power Tactics for the New SAT* series. He has taught and tutored students of all backgrounds and advised both students and parents in preparing for the SAT. Doug graduated magna cum laude from Cornell University in 1992, earning a B.A. in history. He continued his work in the history and sociology of science at the University of Pennsylvania, receiving an M.A. in 1996.

While in graduate school, Doug began teaching SAT test-prep classes. After completing his graduate work, Doug moved to New York City and continued working in test prep, adding PSAT, SCI HI, SAT II: Writing, SAT II: Math, GMAT, and other courses to his repertoire. In 1999, Doug became a curriculum developer, designing instructional material for state proficiency exams.

Doug also writes fiction and poetry. He is an avid drummer, biker, and reader. He currently lives in Metuchen, New Jersey.

SPARKNOTES
Power Tactics for the New SAT

The Critical Reading Section

Reading Passages

Sentence Completions

The Math Section

Algebra

Data Analysis, Statistics & Probability

Geometry

Numbers & Operations

The Writing Section

The Essay

Multiple-Choice Questions: Identifying Sentence Errors,
Improving Sentences, Improving Paragraphs

The New SAT

Test-Taking Strategies

Vocab Builder